The 7N7 Challenge

The 7N7 Challenge, Volume 1

Jeff McCorkle

Published by Jeff McCorkle, 2024.

While every precaution has been taken in the preparation of this book, the publisher assumes no responsibility for errors or omissions, or for damages resulting from the use of the information contained herein.

THE 7N7 CHALLENGE

First edition. October 31, 2024.

Copyright © 2024 Jeff McCorkle.

ISBN: 979-8227658449

Written by Jeff McCorkle.

Table of Contents

Chapter One / The Challenge

The 7N7 Challenge is centered around camping and is designed to push oneself outdoors. I created this challenge for myself, and it quickly consumed a significant portion of my thoughts. Planning, researching, checking the weather, and examining gear became enjoyable because there was a framework and a goal. The camping trips were more satisfying due to the fun of preparation and anticipation. The trips allowed me to assess what worked well and what needed improvement. If you enjoy camping or think you might, but struggle to make time for it, this challenge can motivate you. You deserve to have some time to yourself in the great outdoors.

Challenging yourself or accepting a challenge fosters personal growth. When searching for information on accepting challenges, many results focus on overcoming obstacles. However, these are not true challenges; they are hurdles we face in life. This is not a book about that. Merriam-Webster offers seven definitions for the word "challenge." The one relevant to our topic is: to invite into competition. Here, I invite you, or you can adjust the challenge to suit your situation, to compete against life's pressures, weather conditions, insects, isolation, and ultimately have fun while camping.

The challenge is this: To tent camp in seven North Carolina State Parks in seven months. Ideally, it's best to take one trip per month, but it's not mandatory. The goal is to complete seven different trips in seven different parks over a seven-month period. Simple, right? Not as simple as it may seem. However, it is achievable, especially if you live in or near North Carolina. If not, you can adapt the concept to your region. Everyone's situation is unique, and this challenge may not be feasible for everyone. It will be more challenging for some than for others. For instance, being retired allows me to go during the week when reservations are easier to make. If you work and are limited to weekends, it can be more difficult. But if you love the outdoors and camping, you can do this or adjust it to fit your lifestyle.

To make it a legitimate challenge, there must be rules. For this challenge, the rules are straightforward. Firstly, "camp" refers to camping in a tent. A year or so after this challenge, I got a small teardrop camper. I might adjust future challenges to include it. But you have to draw the line somewhere in order for it to be a real challenge. For example, if you were to travel in a large motorhome, it would hardly be a challenge, as you could complete it in a week without ever leaving the vehicle.

Secondly, you must complete seven camping trips, which is more difficult than it may seem. If you lead a busy life, finding the time and favorable weather conditions can make it challenging to achieve seven trips, even in your backyard. Why seven? While some may attribute significance to the number seven in ancient times, major religions, or mathematics, the truth is, for the casual camper in North Carolina, there are approximately seven months with pleasant weather suitable for camping. I chose April through October as the ideal timeframe. Although there are additional months with favorable camping conditions, the weather in early spring and late fall can be more limited, narrowing the window of opportunity.

Thirdly, the challenge requires camping in seven different North Carolina state parks. This encourages you to explore a variety of locations rather than settling into one familiar spot. Are there seven NC state parks that allow camping? Yes, and each park offers unique features and activities. We will discuss these parks in Chapter Four. You may be pleasantly surprised by the diverse camping experiences North Carolina has to offer.

Fourth and finally, the challenge must be completed within seven months as previously mentioned. You can choose the starting month and continue for seven consecutive months. Although you could double up on one month and skip another, that might detract from the intended fun and excitement of the challenge. Additionally, you can camp for any duration ranging from one night to fourteen. I believe the maximum number of consecutive nights allowed in the same spot is fourteen. Personally, I typically camp for two nights during the middle of the week. Two nights is the minimum reservation period at some parks when booking online, which we will explore further in Chapter Five.

The 7N7 Challenge emerged from my desire to find purpose after retiring at a young age. Although I had plenty to keep me busy managing a Gospel Group and other pursuits, I realized I was investing too much time in these endeavors in an attempt to maintain a sense of importance. This led to neglecting the enjoyable activities I initially intended to pursue in retirement. My background in Boy Scouts, where I learned leadership through camping, played a significant role in my love for the outdoors. I remained involved with the organization into adulthood and eventually became a Scoutmaster. Additionally, my family enjoyed camping during my childhood, instilling a lifelong appreciation for the activity. Over time, my camping experiences evolved from tent camping to using a pop-up camper, travel trailer, and eventually a large Fifth Wheel RV. However, I found the Fifth Wheel to be too overwhelming, prompting me to return to my roots and rediscover my passion for tent camping.

In 2018, I made a conscious decision to devote more time to the enjoyable activities I had initially retired for. As my wife continued to work three days a week, I decided to leave the large camper at home and embark on tent camping trips during the week. I soon realized that a single excursion would not suffice in addressing my need for a meaningful and entertaining hobby. I needed something more involved. I devised the concept of camping in seven state parks in seven months as a challenge to motivate and inspire me and named it 7N7.

;lj0

"What is ';lj0'?" you might ask. Well, it has no meaning. I just cleaned the computer screen and keyboard and when I finished, that is what had been typed by the paper towel. Sounds cool, though.

On a more serious note, I need to insert a disclaimer somewhere and right here might be as good a place as any. Disclaimer: *This book is designed to provide information about tent camping and related activities. However, it is not intended to be a substitute for professional medical advice or diagnosis, or treatment. If you have any pre-existing health conditions or concerns, it is strongly recommended that you consult with your healthcare provider before engaging in any camping activities mentioned in this book. Some camping activities may be physically demanding and could potentially exacerbate certain health issues. Individuals with heart disease, respiratory problems, diabetes, or any other serious medical condition should use extreme caution and consider the risks before embarking on any camping trips. It is the reader's sole responsibility to assess their own physical capabilities and limitations.*

With that out of the way, are you intrigued by the idea of The 7N7 Challenge at this point? Are you prepared to embark on this adventure and have some fun? Are you weary of the daily grind, political strife, and cultural decline? Are you frustrated with relying on modern, high-tech gadgets for entertainment? Tired of being confined indoors with others who share your weariness? It's time for a change of pace. Let's get started. First, we'll need to gather some essential equipment.

Welcome to:
7 N 7
Challenge

Chapter Two / Equipment

As we previously discussed, when I began The 7N7 Challenge, I already had some quality camping gear from my past experiences. If you're an avid camper, you likely possess everything you need to participate. Feel free to skip ahead to Chapter Three, or continue reading; you might come across something new and valuable. For those starting from scratch, knowing what equipment you need can be daunting. In this section, I'll outline my setup and provide a comprehensive list of essential gear.

Interestingly, when I commenced the challenge, I didn't own a tent. I'd had several good ones in the past, but many were loaned out or given away. I was determined to see how little I could spend to get started. I visited my local sporting goods store, where I found a three-man dome tent on sale for $25 right at the entrance. A 3-man tent is spacious enough for one person and gear or two people with minimal belongings.

There are several advantages to using a small, inexpensive tent. They're more affordable, lightweight, and easy to pack. They are also usually simpler to set up, take down, and repack by yourself. Additionally, they provide better warmth than an oversized tent. While I've since upgraded my tent, I am not an expert on the various tent options available. I can only speak to what works best for me. A helpful tip: if you purchase an inexpensive tent, invest in a can of waterproofing spray for around $10 to protect it.

I sifted through my remaining camping equipment, remembering the valuable lesson I learned in Scouts about having a dedicated box or container for kitchen gear. Although I already had a box with the necessary items, it didn't fit easily into the back of my Jeep. To resolve this issue, I measured the available space and purchased a plastic sealable tote. I then filled it with all the cooking essentials and other items that are often required for camping. Here's a list of the basic contents of my box during my first outing:

A Boy Scout Cook kit. (stacking pots, pans and plates) available for around $30 on eBay.

A Boy Scout Cooking Utensil Kit. (Spatulas, knife, etc.) No longer available. Lucky if you find one used.

- Two Enamelware plates.
- Two Enamelware cups
- One plastic dish pan
- Two dish cloths
- One single burner stove
- One or two gas bottles
- One Coleman gas lantern
- One pack of mantels for the lantern
- Two lighters
- Can opener
- One box of Ziploc bags
- One roll of aluminum foil
- One roll of paper towels
- Several Styrofoam plates, bowls
- One pack of playing cards
- One small bottle of dish detergent
- One bar of bath soap
- One square of green scrubbing pad
- One small AM/FM radio

This list encompasses most of the items required for camp cooking, excluding the food itself. I won't delve too deeply into camp cooking, as those who are skilled in the kitchen can adapt their abilities to the outdoor setting with limited burners, counter space, and gadgetry. If cooking isn't your forte, don't worry. You can follow my lead and heat a can of chili beans for dinner and enjoy sandwiches or snacks for the other meals. Customize your camping experience to suit your preferences. And, speaking of snacks, feel free to indulge on your camping trip. It's a vacation, after all, and you have my permission to enjoy a few extra treats.

When planning your meals, pack food in a separate container. Store this container in your car when not in use or, if available, utilize the heavy metal food storage lockers installed at some mountain campgrounds. This helps prevent attracting bears, although raccoons pose a more common threat. A raccoon can easily create chaos in a camp kitchen, so proper food storage is crucial.

I feel the need to expand on meal planning. I suppose there are numerous methods to this but I'll give you my system and you can adjust it as necessary. First, I decide which meals and how many I will need to prepare for. For a two-night trip, that equals two suppers, two breakfasts and two lunches. And never underestimate the need to pack some snacks. Oh, and don't forget drinks.

I then decide what I want to fix for each meal and make a full list of ingredients needed. Next, I look around my own kitchen to scavenge as many of the items as I can. This saves money. Sometimes I will have everything I need. More times than not, I have to make a shopping trip.

Once I get everything together, I place all of the non-refrigerated items in a cheap soft-sided cooler that I use for this purpose, since it is good for nothing else and was a free promotional item. Your standard ice tea class would keep ice better than that thing. I check everything off my previously crafted list as I pack it. I then pack the actual cooler I'm using with the refrigerated items and check them off the list.

This system works good for me. I don't always have everything I need when I get to camp but I usually have everything I had placed on my list. The things I am missing usually never got put on the list. Your food packing list is only as good as the thoroughness of your mind allows it to be.

Next on my list was sleeping gear. I had two suitable sleeping bags: a decent inexpensive bag for milder temperatures and a military surplus cocoon bag rated for colder weather. Although these military bags used to be affordable, they now cost over $150. I always bring both bags with me. I don't like sleeping on the ground. By that I mean directly on the tent floor. I have become soft and spoiled. The closest thing I can come up with to meet my old-man comfort needs is an air mattress. I had a single-sized one which I purchased from Walmart. It has proven durable, as I used it twice a week for two years while caring for my mother, and I still use the same one today. Air mattresses are easy to find at any sporting goods store, and proper care is key to their longevity. I also packed my own pillow from home for added comfort.

A reliable flashlight is essential, and I recommend having at least two on hand, in addition to a lantern. I initially used a couple of random flashlights and a gas lantern, which proved invaluable on the first night. It's always good to have a backup flashlight, since one is likely to fail when you need it most. Nowadays, it's helpful to have an LED strap-on headlamp for hands-free convenience.

It is always a good thing to have a chair to sit in. Just any old folding canvas yard chair will work. I usually take one of those and a gravity lounger that is good for naps. If you are younger and want to pack light, you might forgo the chair. You will regret it. If you don't treat yourself nice, nobody else will. Take a chair.

If you intend to cook on a grill, it is advisable to bring your own. Although a grill might be present at the campsite as part of the fire ring, its functionality cannot be guaranteed and the leftover food substance stuck to it might be from a questionable origin. Should you prefer cooking over the fire, be sure to pack the necessary utensils, such as skewers - the sticks commonly used by Southerners to cook hot dogs and by Yankees to make s'mores.

Tent camping can be an expensive endeavor, but it doesn't have to be. Often, items associated with camping are priced higher solely due to their association with backpacking. A fork, for instance, remains a fork regardless of its intended use. An entry-level camping fork and spoon set at a big box chain store can cost over $12, while in the kitchen section, a set of four stainless steel forks is available for $1.26. Alternatively, one can simply use a fork from home. This example illustrates the manipulative nature of pricing. While spending $12 on a fork set may not be an issue, it highlights the way the game is rigged. Simplicity is often the best approach.

And don't get me started on overpriced coolers. For a two-night camping trip for two people, you need about a twenty-quart cooler. For longer stays, you might need a larger one. Of course, the cheaper ones do not hold ice for as long as the overpriced ones. There are ways to make coolers function more efficiently. Pre-cool it, pack 2/3 ice to 1/3 food, keep it closed, and most importantly, keep it in the shade. The campground sells ice. I have not had to buy any from them yet.

I use the term "overpriced" instead of "expensive" because certain modern coolers are over-engineered for their intended purpose, and some are marketed as status symbols. I see no need to overpay for a cooler merely to advertise their product with a sticker on my truck window. I've discovered that utilizing a five-gallon water cooler, yes, the ugly orange one, as a camping cooler works effectively and retains ice marginally longer than a standard square one. Additionally, it is advisable to avoid soft-sided coolers entirely. Ultimately, there is no necessity for a 100-quart cooler that preserves ice (four bags of it) for five days for a two-day trip.

When tent camping you need some type of water container. You can pick up a five to seven-gallon water container for around $12 to $15. Or you can rinse out a couple gallon milk jugs and fill them up at home and refill them at the campgrounds water source. You will need about five gallons for a two-night camping trip for two people, more if the weather is exceptionally hot.

Minimum gear campsite / Lake James

A word about firewood: North Carolina state parks and parks in other states as well, do not want you to bring your own firewood or move firewood from place to place. They are concerned about the Emerald Ash Borer. Here is the statement from their website:

Please do not transport firewood into our state parks, because you could unknowingly spread dangerous insects and diseases, such as the emerald ash borer, which can harm the natural resources. Buy firewood locally where you intend to burn it, or buy heat-treated firewood. Visit the Don't Move Firewood website[1] for more information on how to have a risk-free campfire experience. All state parks with camping areas sell firewood at either the park office or visitor center, or the concession stand, or through the campground host.

The statement refers you to the Don't Move Firewood website. The site provides useful information on the topic. If you were to study the subject closely, as I have, you could come to the conclusion that the problem is not as serious as they make it out to be. However, I don't advise bringing your own firewood from home. I also don't advise buying firewood from the park. In my experience, it isn't seasoned and doesn't start or burn very well. According to the guidelines, you can bring store-bought wood which has been kiln dried. That will burn better than wood from the campground. Either way, the best way to get stubborn wood to burn is to split it down to very small pieces. You'll need an ax or hatchet for that, and a first aid kit.

I like to pack light. I bring essential items and even some nonessential "luxuries". The goal is to keep it simple enough that you can keep your gear at one location at home. Then you can toss it in the vehicle when you are ready to go, knowing you aren't having to remember every item because everything is kept together.

Here's a basic list of what you will need:

- Tent
- Sleeping bag
- Sleeping pad or air mattress

---

1. *https://www.dontmovefirewood.org/*

- Pillow (optional)
- Adequate clothing and something to carry and store it in
- Rain coat or poncho
- Toiletries
- Sun screen, sun glasses
- Bath towel
- Chair (optional)
- Ax or hatchet to split firewood
- Lighter (more than one)
- Lantern, battery or gas
- Fuel for Lantern
- Flashlight x2
- Knife
- Kitchen fly or canopy (optional)
- Cooking stove
- Fuel for Cooking Stove
- Cooking utensils
- Pots, pans
- Cooler (see comments above)
- Food
- Water
- Dish soap
- Water container
- Eating utensils
- Plates, cups, bowls
- Aluminum foil
- Small plastic bags for trash
- Paper towels
- Dish towel
- Dish rag
- Scrubber
- Plastic table cloth (optional)

- First Aid Kit
- Insect repellent
- Firewood (see comments)

Chapter Three / First Time Out

We're going to cover all the information about camping, parks, activities, and other exciting aspects. First, I want to share my first camping experience in this challenge, highlighting the potential obstacles you may face. Hopefully, it will also reflect the absolute fun and excitement a memorable camping trip can create.

By mid-April 2018, I had cleaned up my old gear, purchased a few new items, and was ready to begin the challenge. I packed everything into the back of my Jeep Wrangler, kissed my wife goodbye, and headed to Lake Norman State Park, a convenient location less than thirty minutes from my home. I booked two nights online. The weather was clear and cool, and despite my wife's concerns about the dropping temperatures, I was bundled up and determined to continue. This camping trip was shaping up to be one of the most exciting excursions I had experienced, as it was my first time in a very long time going completely alone, aside from backyard camping.

All packed up for the first time out

Upon arrival, I proceeded directly to the site. Since that first trip, I've learned that check-in procedures vary across North Carolina parks, changing depending on the park and season. On this occasion, the policy was to set up camp first and a ranger would come by to check me in. The Park Ranger stopped by shortly after I set up camp. After she left, it was suddenly very peaceful and quiet. And, lonely in a good way. I took a minute to just look around with excitement in the crisp air.

Leaving behind old frustrations and embracing new concerns, I pitched my cheap little tent. I stowed my gear inside, set up my camp kitchen and took a look around. It was already getting cooler. There were about four or five other campers in the park. My nearest neighbor was two sites away. She had no tent and appeared to be staying in her car, occasionally practicing yoga and chanting unintelligibly. I never saw her set up any type of camp, which struck me as peculiar. The campers on the other side of her had a tent, and further along, some folks were staying in an old RV. These were the only occupants at the park

As the temperature continued to drop, the wind picked up. Earlier, when the Park Ranger checked me in, she inquired if I needed to purchase firewood. I declined. I didn't tell her I had my own because there are some sketchy rules about firewood. I started a fire and began getting my food ready to cook. I started early because I didn't want to clean up the dishes in the dark. I began to wonder if I had enough wood to stay warm.

I had brought some charcoal, using it alongside a small fire within the fire ring. I prepared a half-pound of ground beef, diced potatoes, carrots, onions, and ample butter, seasoned with salt and pepper, and wrapped it in aluminum foil. Placing it on the charcoal, I cooked it for about 20 to 30 minutes on each side. This is an old standard camping meal from my scouting days that really hits the spot.

After finishing the meal and tidying up, I decided to take a walk. I never encountered the Park Ranger again. During peak camping season, each park has a camp host who is staying in the campground and can provide firewood. However, there was no camp host present for this early in the year. My concern for the limited supply of firewood sent me looking in vacant campsites. I located several good sticks of wood left behind by previous campers, so I made a mental note of the locations. I went back later after it started to get dark and brought them to my site. THIS IS A "No-no". As I said, there are some peculiar firewood rules so don't do as I do, do as I say. I felt like in this particular case my little foray into criminal misconduct would have to be overlooked since there was no longer anyone around to sell me wood.

I bundled up in a fleece hoodie and spent the rest of the evening relaxing by the fire. The cold wind coming off the water, up the slope to my campsite was, for a time overshadowed by the spectacular sunset through the trees over the lake. I was staying relatively warm on the side facing the fire, but a bit cold on the backside. I still had a M-65 army field jacket, including the winter liner, up my sleeve... so to speak. That's a good piece of equipment to have, by the way. However, for the time being, I was comfortable with the layers I had on.

When I say it got cold, I should clarify that it was coooold for me. I tend to feel cold all winter living in the south, so my tolerance for cold is not very high. Many of you might argue that what I experienced wasn't particularly cold, and that's true when compared to the standards of others. However, for this old man's bones, it was super cold.

Regardless of the cold, the experience was fantastic. The picturesque view, stunning sunset, peaceful surroundings, and the initial feeling of accomplishment allowed all external worries to dissipate. It is an ideal way to unwind, clear your mind, and rejuvenate your heart. An hour after the final rays of sunset faded away, I loaded the last piece of wood on the fire and watched it burn and crackle until the flames finally died out. I grabbed the lantern and headed to the little tent.

I had already inflated my air mattress and placed my sleeping bags on it. I can't sleep with my bed completely leveled or with my head lower than the rest of my body, as it causes dizziness. The ground is always somewhat tilted, even on a level tent pad at a campground. It's not always easy to determine which end is higher. To address this, I invented a unique trick. I laid a water bottle on the mattress lengthwise, and the end where the air bubble migrated to indicated the higher side.

The less expensive sleeping bag was not warm enough on its own. I unzipped it and placed the military bag inside. While doing this, I kept the gas lantern on, being cautious with it. This is another "no-no", using a gas lantern inside a small tent. However, it effectively warmed the tent as I removed excess clothing. I climbed into the inner bag and covered my head with the field jacket. I reached out of the bundle, turned off the lantern and tried to sleep. It didn't take long for the tent to cool down from the lantern's heat, and the bed to warm up from my body heat. For me, sleeping in a warm bed while it's colder outside is the most restful sleep one can experience.

Even though I slept very well, the sounds of the night were quite audible in the tent. Camping in a tent exposes you to a variety of nighttime noises, some soothing and others rather spooky. The wind was a constant presence, traveling across the lake in waves, rustling the trees, and eventually shaking the tent. This made me wonder just how cold it was outside of that warm bag. I could hear various animals moving about, with one in particular getting progressively closer. The more you think about something like that the more dangerous the animal becomes in your mind. Whatever it was, small and harmless I'm sure, it eventually moved on. Next thing I knew it was daylight and I was fully awake.

Being snug in a warm bed makes it hard to rouse yourself on a cold morning. You tend to delay the inevitable exposure to the cold air and getting dressed for as long as you can. Eventually, the call of nature forces you up and out. Just before making the move, I remembered the gas lantern. I reached out, ignited it and waited about five minutes. By then the tent was nice and toasty and I climbed out and got dressed and headed out to greet the day.

I broke out the frying pan and fried up a quick bacon and egg breakfast, eating it while standing over the stove, relishing the heat it emitted. The food cooled before I could finish it but it really hit the spot. I cleaned up the kitchen and buttoned up the camp. I needed to either go back home or run into town for some firewood and a couple of forgotten items. I decided to stop somewhere for a cup of coffee instead of trying to make my own in camp. Attempting to make my own seemed futile due to the cold. I hopped into the Jeep to let it warm up, and in doing so, warmed myself. I then noticed that the yoga practitioner and other campers had departed, leaving me as the only one bold enough to remain overnight.

I sent my wife a text update, assuring her that all was well. She expressed relief and provided the overnight low temperature in the nearest city, twenty-nine degrees. Given that this was the temperature in town, it was likely a few degrees colder at the campsite, exacerbated by the chilling lake wind.

I got out and about in the Jeep. I got some coffee and headed to Mooresville with no place in particular in mind. This came to be a customary aspect of my trips. That is, to tour the area in search of some interesting old country store or local point of interest. I picked up a couple bundles of wood at a farm supply store and returned to camp.

I needed to get some exercise. I saw a hiking trail that went by my campsite. I got on it and hiked for approximately half an hour before turning back, uncertain of where it would end. The trail, known as the Lake Shore Trail, clung to the shoreline and offered excellent views of both the woods and the lake. I later discovered that it is a five-mile loop, one of fifteen trails within the park. Some trails are designated for hiking only, while others accommodate both hiking and mountain biking. Lake Norman State Park is an excellent choice for anyone interested in either activity, as well as for those just beginning their exploration of these pursuits. I have returned many times for a day hike.

The weather grew warmer and the breeze subsided. I did some more exploring in the park then settled in for a chair nap. If you've never taken a nap outdoors in a chair, you've been missing out. The sounds of birds singing, leaves ruffling in the breeze, squirrels chattering, and distant waves lapping at the shoreline all work in orchestration to create a tranquilizing effect. Before you know it, you have experienced a session of true relaxation. Key point here... don't sleep with your mouth open.

I had brought my banjo along on the trip. Following my nap, I got it out and tuned it up. I found a sizable stump in the woods behind my campsite and sat down on it facing the lake and cut loose on all the bluegrass standards. It enhances your playing when you can really dig into the songs knowing that likely no one can hear you. Interestingly, I have since discovered on numerous camping trips that people do, in fact, hear the music. They often approach me later to compliment my playing. I have observed that while most people claim to genuinely appreciate banjo music, their interest drops off rapidly after the first song or two.

On a two-night camping trip I enjoy light lunches and usually plan one supper meal and one breakfast meal that require some cooking skills. That leaves one of each that is simple to prepare. For my second evening I had the easy meal, which ended up being a can of chili beans. I cooked them in a small pot and ate them directly from the pot to minimize dishwashing. Still just as tasty. Enhancing it with a sprinkling of corn chips and grated cheese created a delightful, effortless meal to savor around the campfire. This meal prompted me to make a mental note for a purchase for the next trip. That was a compact, non-stick frying pan measuring approximately eight inches in diameter. Ideal for a single person, it serves as an appropriate vessel for heating (and eating) canned food like chili beans or stew, and is remarkably easy to clean.

The temperature had warmed up nicely. I found myself seated by the small campfire enjoying the chili beans while observing the sun embark on its gradual descent. I had tuned the AM/FM radio to a nearby Southern Gospel station. After finishing the satisfying meal, the warmth of the fire and the picturesque surroundings settled my soul into a peace that is difficult to describe. I neither admit to, nor advocate indulging in anything harmful. However, if you are a person who enjoys the occasional indulgence of a fine cigar, insert that into your mind for this story right about here.

As I reflected on the journey, I recognized that I had achieved and encountered more than I had initially hoped. Experiencing the peaceful outdoors, successfully overcoming the challenging weather conditions and proving to myself that I could handle it individually, made me glad I came. It also further fueled my determination to continue the challenge and start planning the next adventure.

After the fire died out, I repeated the nighttime routine and slept like a baby for the final night of my trip. Although check-out wasn't required until midday, I am always ready to get packing as soon as I get up and have breakfast. This I did, packing up my little tent and all my gear. As always, I made a last check of the site for anything left behind including any bits of litter no matter how small. This is simply good policy.

I headed home to stow my gear, indulge in a much-needed shower, and get on with life. I have cultivated the habit of ensuring all of the camping equipment is packed away clean and ready for the next trip. That includes airing out the sleeping bags even if you don't think they were exposed to any moisture. If the tent got any moisture at all, it is best to lay it out in the sun to dry out completely before you pack it away. Yes, even a cheap one.

I took good care of this cheap tent and used it about eight or ten trips and it never failed me. When I upgraded, I gave it to someone who continued to use it without issue.

Another habit I adopted involves storing all the ready-to-go gear together so that it is really easy to pack next time. It also helps to prevent you from forgetting and leaving essential items behind.

I enjoyed the trip immensely. This is one that will always stand out to me for whatever reason. I suspect my storytelling prowess fails to explain how much fun this first trip of the challenge was for me. The park was a good choice and an easy one for me. As my challenge continued, the task of selecting destinations became increasingly difficult, necessitating thorough research. Fortunately, for future 7N7 participants, I have undertaken much of this preparatory groundwork. In the next section, we will delve into the array of park choices available.

Chapter Four / Parks

I'll start with a word of praise about North Carolina state parks. In general, they are exceptionally well-managed. Having experienced parks in other states, I have often been left disappointed. I am certain that there are states that have parks that match the quality of North Carolina, but I have not personally encountered any. National Parks, too, are well-managed, but I believe the standard of North Carolina state parks surpasses even that. However, it is possible that I am slightly biased.

From my home in central North Carolina, accessing numerous parks with camping facilities is fairly convenient. The Division of Parks and Recreation oversees these state parks. This division is also responsible for managing natural areas, trails, lakes, natural and scenic rivers, and recreational areas. Additionally, they are in charge of the North Carolina Trails System, the North Carolina Natural and Scenic Rivers and the Parks and Recreation Trust Fund. The division also assists other recreation providers by offering grant programs for park and trail projects.

There are approximately forty-four state parks, with some being referred to as "recreation areas" or "natural areas". Out of these, twenty-nine parks offer various camping facilities. There are several types of camping facilities. There are Tent and/or RV campgrounds which are what I call "drive-to" campgrounds. There are backpacking camping facilities that, of course, are not drive-to. There are Paddle-in camping areas that are accessible only by water. There are Equestrian campgrounds that are rich with features for those who ride horses. There are some Group campgrounds and some campgrounds have cabins available. Some parks have a mixture of these. For the purpose of our discussions, we will focus on the drive-to tent camping facilities. However, individuals may choose to create challenges involving other types of camping facilities as well.

By my estimation, there are twenty-two parks that offer drive-to tent camping facilities. I have personally camped in ten of them and visited several others. In this account, I will relate my experiences at the ten parks I have visited, providing a diverse selection for a 7N7 Challenge. My goal is to explore the remaining parks in future challenges, potentially leading to a second publication. The second trip on my original challenge took me to Pilot Mountain State Park.

Pilot Mountain State Park

Pilot Mountain is situated northwest of Winston Salem, North Carolina. The park encompasses multiple sections and access points, offering a variety of activities in addition to camping, such as fourteen miles of hiking trails, nine miles of horseback riding trails, and access to the Yadkin River. The focal point of the park is the mountain itself. Pilot Mountain is a monadnock, which is a mountain or rock mass that has withstood erosion, causing it to stand out among relatively flat surrounding landscape. (My definition. Not bad huh?). In this case the pinnacle bears a striking resemblance to a ship's pilothouse, giving the mountain its name. https://www.ncparks.gov/state-parks/pilot-mountain-state-park

At the summit of Pilot Mountain, there is a picturesque area where visitors can park, enjoy the views, and hike. This feature is very popular on weekends and causes long lines of vehicles waiting to get in. The primary entrance to this parking area also serves as the main road leading to the campground. To alleviate congestion during peak season, a shuttle service is provided. The traffic situation makes it advisable to visit this park during the week. Also, the campground is closed from December through February. It's a great place to camp, but planning is essential when visiting this park.

Sumit Overlook / Pilot Mountain State Park

Upon establishing your campsite, you will have direct access to the Grindstone Trail, which connects you to all the trails in the Mountain Section. A word of caution is in order here. Some of the hiking trails in the Mountain section are strenuous, especially if you take the Grindstone Trail or the Ledge Spring Trail to the summit. Warning signs are posted that include wording that will put the fear in you if you are not in the best shape physically. I think it's a good idea to keep in mind that it is supposed to be fun. You don't always have to complete every trail you start. There is no shame in turning around at a good halfway point for you so that you can enjoy the walk.

In the Yadkin River section, there are hiking and horse trails which can only be accessed from that section of the park. Additionally, a paddle launch and paddle-in camping facilities are available for use. Plan ahead if you want to use these features.

As previously mentioned, I like to scout out the local area for interesting things. The neighboring town is also called Pilot Mountain.

It is rich in history and has a nice hometown feel about it as you travel through the quaint downtown area. Some believe that the fictional town of "Mount Pilot" in the Andy Griffith Show is inspired by this town. Nearby towns of Mt. Airy, Dobson and King all have interesting shops and attractions. The region features guided mountain climbing and horseback riding, ziplines, wineries, antiques and old country stores. Part of the fun is discovering these activities and more through your own explorations.

Fall leaf-watching is popular in this area. That activity can sometime increase the congestion into the park. Various local festivals are held in neighboring towns, providing additional entertainment options. If you really want a scenic drive, you can access the Blue Ridge Parkway, thirty-five miles away. If you do, check out Mt. Airy on the way.

During my stay at Pilot Mountain, I had the pleasure of meeting the camp hosts, a couple employed by the park. It pays to speak to these folks. They can provide valuable information about park activities and local attractions. As fellow campers they understand the way of life and what you need. It gives you a sense of security knowing folks like that are available to assist in case of an emergency.

In addition to exploring the local antique scene, I embarked on hikes during both days of my stay at Pilot Mountain. On the second day I braved my way past the scary warning signs and headed up to the summit. It was exhausting but the breathtaking views from the peak were well worth the effort. I looked around the parking area for some friendly face to ask for a ride back down. After a while, I eventually realized that if I had driven to the top and seen someone looking like me begging a ride, I would decline. So, I rested up and headed back. Downhill can be as strenuous as uphill if it comes as the second half of a hike. I made it back and thanked God that I was still healthy enough to experience that hike and the scenery that it revealed.

Pilot Mountain is an enjoyable park for camping. I enjoyed my visit there. Before the challenge, I had been a visitor in that area many times over the years but never camped there. If you prefer a variety of activities within the park and its vicinity, coupled with a serene, shaded campsite, Pilot Mountain is a nice option. Where to next? It's not too far up the road to Hanging Rock.

Hanging Rock State Park

Getting a camping trip scheduled each month is challenging, even for a retiree. There always seems to be a conflict with other activities. Finding a break in the enterprise of daily life is not enough; the weather also needs to cooperate. Eventually, everything aligned, allowing for a trip toward the end of June. I decided to visit Hanging Rock Park, which is a bit further from my home but easily accessible. It is thirty miles north of Winston Salem, NC. https://www.ncparks.gov/state-parks/hanging-rock-state-park

The park offers various recreational activities, including hiking, biking, and horseback riding on its various trails. In addition, there is a lake for swimming and paddle boating. The park's central attraction is the peak of the rock outcropping. There, you can enjoy spectacular views and rest from the climb.

Nearby, there is access to the Dan River, which is great for canoeing, kayaking and tubing. The tiny town of Danbury offers local shops and tube rentals. I ventured out on my second day to find the river access in Danbury, which features picnic tables and restrooms. It is an ideal spot to relax, observe the water, and watch people pass by. The local area is very scenic for people like me and who like to poke around and explore.

I ventured a few miles outside of town to visit the Historic Priddy's General Store, which has been in operation for over 100 years. I arrived just as a Bible study was concluding on the front porch, where most social activities occur. I spoke to the folks and excused myself inside to get a soft drink and a snack. The store offers a mix of vintage merchandise and modern essentials. The folks running it are as warm and friendly as you would expect from such an inviting, laid back, off-the-beaten-path spot.

Back out on the porch I was peppered with questions from the guys hanging out. The conversation inevitably turned to bluegrass music and camping. We chatted for some time before I decided to head back to camp. The old store is worth taking in. Other than the "old" part, it's no different than the stores we always had around my home stomping grounds as I was growing up. They weren't called convenience stores then. "Curb Market" was the term used around home. They are becoming a thing of the past. So am I, I guess.

The only hiking trail accessible from the campground is Moore's Wall Loop, a challenging 4.7-mile loop that intersects with other trails. To reach the mountain's summit, you'll need the Hanging Rock Trail, which begins at the Visitors Center's parking lot. Your best bet is to drive, or walk if you feel energetic, and start there. Save your strength. The trail is a 1.3-mile "out and back" journey, totaling 2.6 miles. It starts with a pleasant, level gravel path, giving the impression of an easy walk. However, it becomes more challenging after a few hundred yards, and though it is classified as moderate, I would consider it to be on the strenuous end of that spectrum.

Upon reaching the summit, the overlook provides panoramic views spanning over 180 degrees The area is composed of rocks and uneven terrain, with several dangerous edges and drop-offs. Those with a fear of heights may find this unsettling. If there are kids running around the rocky area, it will make it a lot worse. They are excited and lack a sense of safety. Even adults sometimes recklessly approach the edge for a view, thrill, or photograph. There are no barriers. Tragically, there have been fatalities. However, there is ample space to enjoy the views without venturing near the hazardous edges.

Back at camp as I began to heat my easy meal of the trip, I heard a rustling and looked up to see a deer grazing at the edge of the campsite. The deer didn't regard me at all and munched on the foliage the entire time I cooked. Such a sight after the exhausting hike, made for a peaceful evening.

Friendly Deer / Hanging Rock State Park

I have camped at Hanging Rock on multiple occasions. It is a great place to camp for the active person, yet offers peaceful surroundings for those who prefer camping for relaxation. I have enjoyed it both ways there. Plan ahead if you want to participate in the various activities so that you will bring the proper gear. Now it's time to venture toward the mountainous western part of the state.

Lake James State Park

As the temperatures rise in North Carolina, folks tend to seek refuge in the cooler climate of the hills. July came around, and I decided to do the same. I chose Lake James State Park. This park is divided into two sections: Paddy's Creek and Catawba River. The park has many features and is a popular place to beat the heat. https://www.ncparks.gov/state-parks/lake-james-state-park

There are three separate camping areas available. First, the Catawba River Campground offers lakeside, walk-in camping. Parking facilities are conveniently located nearby, and a bathhouse is situated in close proximity to the parking area. Secondly, Long Arm Campground provides three sections of paddle-in / boat-in camping. If you want to try that experience, and don't have the proper vessel, the park may rent you one, provided it's between the first of April and the end of October. Lastly, the Paddy's Creek drive-to campground features thirty-three sites, complete with a bathhouse. That's the one we want.

Lake James Paddy's Creek Entrance

Lake James offers both hiking and biking trails, with some designated for dual-use and others exclusively for hiking. All trails are classified as easy or moderate in difficulty. And, of course, there are lake activities of fishing, boating, and paddling. A nice beach area is available for swimming, complete with a bathhouse and concession stand, typically opening for the season around May 1st.

The park's website indicates its location to be fifty miles northeast of Asheville. However, there are several interesting towns situated closer to the park. As you head out towards Marion, twenty or so miles away, you will pass through the small, unincorporated town of Nebo. In this area, you can discover guided kayak tours of the lake, antique shops, wineries, and other attractions.

Marion features a vibrant downtown area with shops, dining and local heritage sites. Seasonally, there is a farmer's market downtown known as the Tailgate Market that is worth visiting. It is only open on certain days. Most standard retail stores can be found in the area so if you forgot to bring something for your trip, you can most likely find it. I have done just that: forgotten something, and found it in Marion. Once you make it to Marion, you will find yourself on the I40 corridor, where you have easy access to numerous other mountain towns.

Back in the park, the swimming is fine. The hiking is good. The scenery is great. If you want to hike from the campground, Mill's Creek Trail is right there. It is a moderate 3.6-mile loop. It is possible to extend this hike by accessing the Paddy's Creek Trail, a one-mile out-and-back route that meanders along the shoreline. If you like a little Revolutionary War history with your hike, the Overmountain Victory Trail runs through the park.

The Overmountain Victory National Historic Trail spans 330 miles across North Carolina, South Carolina, Virginia, and Tennessee. This trail commemorates the 1780 route taken by Patriot militia during the crucial Kings Mountain campaign. Although most of the route is designed for driving, there are eighty-seven miles of walkable pathways available. One of those is the easy trail that runs through Lake James State Park. More information can be found on the National Park Service Website https://www.nps.gov/ovvi/planyourvisit/places.htm .

Overall, I enjoyed my visit to Lake James State Park. The area is rich in those old things that I like to tract down. The park can get congested during summer weekends, primarily around the swimming area. I would like to go again sometime, when I am not being lazy, and participate in more of the park's activities. The prospect of paddle-to camping is especially interesting, though I may need to refine my paddling skills first. There may be another challenge involved in the future. The park is well maintained as are most North Carolina parks. It's easily accessible, and conveniently located near essential amenities.

In terms of planning, visitors should simply consider the seasonal availability of certain activities. With four parks now completed, we are more than halfway through our challenge. Next stop, Morrow Mountain.

Morrow Mountain State Park

Morrow Mountain State Park is situated approximately fifty miles northeast of Charlotte, and just a few miles from Albemarle. The park is conveniently located just outside the town of Badin, North Carolina. It borders the Yadkin River and its wider section known as Lake Tillery. It has a boat ramp and boat rentals. Nearby Badin Lake also offers water recreation activity. There are good kayaking waters near the park. Notably, Morrow Mountain is one of the few state parks to feature a swimming pool, despite its lakeside location. https://www.ncparks.gov/state-parks/morrow-mountain-state-park

In terms of camping facilities, Morrow Mountain State Park offers a group camping area, a hike-to campsite, and a drive-to campground featuring tent and RV sites with electricity. The sites are decent and mostly shady. Additionally, there are camping cabins available within the campground, as well as a family vacation cabin situated outside the campground area. I'm not sure how that works. Admittedly, I am not a fan of cabins in campgrounds. I may give my thoughts on it later without going down that rabbit trail here. The campground is fairly centrally located in the park making it easy to access the other activities.

Morrow Mountain State Park offers a variety of activities for visitors, including hiking and horseback trails, facilities for gatherings and events, picnic shelters, and a scenic mountaintop area showcasing the park's natural beauty. For history enthusiasts, there is the Dr. Kron homestead including the original house from the mid 1800's and associated buildings, all with informational displays. Also, a museum at the park office has interesting displays and information about the area.

Dr. Kron Homestead / Morrow Mountain State Park

When you leave the park to go scouting about, you will go through the quaint town of Badin, where you'll find a small selection of shops, stores, and eateries. The town also offers a disc golf course and a beach area along Badin Lake for swimming. If you forgot something not typically found in a dollar store, you may or may not find it in Badin. You likely will find it a few miles away in Albemarle, NC. There you can find most popular chain stores and restaurants. They also have some antique malls and a decent downtown area. There are a couple of sporting goods stores that might have the hard-to-find camping items you inadvertently left at home.

Back at the park, you can access an easy hiking trail that leads directly to the pool if you're seeking some post-nap exercise. If you just want to hike and not get wet, you can use the Rocks Trail. That's a 2.3-mile out-to-the-river-and-back trail. It too is rated easy and it joins the Long

Loop Trail for a while before it separates again before the river. Long Loop is a hiking AND bridle trail so might want to watch where you step. There are several other hiking and bridle trails in the park that do not intersect with the campground.

One of the park's standout features is the overlook area atop Morrow Mountain. Visitors can choose to drive to the summit or hike via the 2.6-mile (moderate) Morrow Mountain Trail, which extends over five miles round-trip with a few inclines. There is ample parking at the overlook, as well as restrooms and a short trail around the summit for fun. The views are great. It's very peaceful at this spot. We have visited this area several times. When we are in this area doing other things, we try to make a stop by here just to relax for a minute.

I thoroughly enjoy camping at Morrow Mountain State Park, as it is conveniently located approximately an hour from my home. I am familiar with the Albemarle area and I grew up with scouting experiences at nearby Camp Barnhardt. The campground is tranquil and well-maintained. Having already explored most of the park's offerings, I plan to return to experience some kayaking. If you like this area, you can also find additional camping and off-roading opportunities in the nearby Uhawarrie National Forest, close to Badin.

Stone Mountain State Park

Stone Mountain State Park is located sixty miles northwest of Winston Salem, with the nearest towns of notable size being Elkin and Sparta. The park surrounds its main feature, a 600-foot granite dome, that has been designated a National Natural Landmark. The park features the characteristic landscape of North Carolina's mountains, complete with waterfalls, creeks, and trout streams. https://www.ncparks.gov/state-parks/stone-mountain-state-park

The park is also home to a restored mid-19th-century farm, the Hutchinson Homestead situated at the base of the mountain. While the homestead is only open for visits on weekends from May through October, the grounds may still be explored when the site is closed. Additionally, the park contains the Garden Creek Baptist Church Historic Site, which hosts services at 9 AM every Sunday during the warmer months and once a month during winter. Visitors are welcome to stroll the church grounds when services are not in session.

The camping situation is somewhat unique for state parks. There is hike-to camping in the backpacking area. The main drive-to campground offers group camping, tent sites with no hookups and RV sites with power and water hookups and a dump station. Thankfully, the park has refrained from constructing any creepy camping cabins. While some parks have sites for tent camping that also have power, and/or water for RVs, this campground has two separate sections, one for tent camping and one for RV. Each section has its own bathhouse.

The great thing about this setup is the availability for tent camping. At the time of this writing, which is post-pandemic, RV camping has experienced a huge surge in popularity. People got tired of being cooped up at home, I guess. This has generated several negative effects. One is that the demand for RVs has led to skyrocketing sales, prompting manufacturers to increase production and, in some cases, compromise on quality. The other problem is campgrounds have become increasingly congested, making reservations at sought-after locations challenging to secure. This is all slowing down some now, and many are having buyer's remorse for various reasons. The good thing for us is, RVers keep the RV section booked up, even during the week. But while that section is full, that usually leaves tent campers with the advantage of a separate section largely undisturbed by RVs, even during peak camping periods.

In addition to the exhibits, visitors can also explore designated trails for both hiking and horseback riding. A segment of North Carolina's renowned Mountains-to-Sea State Trail winds through the park. The trail meanders for 1175 miles from the Great Smoky Mountains all the way to the Outer Banks, with stops at many of the state's most beautiful and interesting places. https://mountainstoseatrail.org

If you are into rock climbing, they have several hike-to locations at Stone Mountain. You'll need to get a permit from the park staff and keep it with you.

There are many stocked trout fishing streams in the area and some in the park. Make sure you have the appropriate license.

The park's interconnected hiking trails provide access to various points of interest, although none can be directly accessed from the campground. By crossing from the campground entrance to the Upper Trailhead parking area, you can access the Stone Mountain Loop Trail which will get you to the summit, eventually. It is somewhat difficult and is a 4.5-mile loop, and designated as strenuous. If you can manage it, the hike is worth the effort to experience the top of a striking granite mountain. For those who prefer a less arduous hike, you can take a left on the trail from the parking lot and hike the "view" side of the loop and see the mountain from the bottom and return. This leads to a nice grassy area that will invite you to sit for a while and take it all in.

Hutchinson Homestead / Stone Mountain State Park

After the hike, you might choose to venture into town for some exploring or picking up supplies. Several small communities surrounding the park offer country stores stocked with essential items. The town of Elkin is about twenty miles downhill and has a Walmart and Lowes and several chain stores and restaurants. They have a downtown area with a few shops, a mural hike and a walking tour. Additionally, the town borders the Yadkin River and offers a kayak access for those seeking some paddling time.

For an uphill journey, consider heading to Sparta, located about fifteen miles away via the curvy and moderately steep US 21. Sparta offers a variety of retail stores, shops, and restaurants, as well as a pleasant downtown area. This route provides a more scenic alternative than the drive to Elkin. On your return trip, be sure to stop at the overlook to take in the long-range views. Also, there is access to the Blue Ridge Parkway on this section of US 21.

My family once owned a vacation home near the park in Traphill, NC. My father enjoyed traveling the roads in the area just to see where they ended up. I was along for some of those excursions and I inherited his passion for exploration. This area is rich in good old county folk, many of whom I have come to know personally. It is a very uplifting part of the world to visit and get away from the hustle and bustle. If you ever wanted to just pick a road to travel for the sole purpose of finding where it goes, this is the place to start. It should be noted, however, that the region once held the distinction of being the unofficial moonshine capital of the world, so be careful and mind your own business.

The park is undeniably beautiful. It is a prime location for fall leaf watching. The granite mountain itself is a spectacular sight visible from below or experienced up close through a challenging hike to the summit. The campground is really nice and the set up with the separate sections makes it great for our type of camping. Having extensive knowledge of the surrounding area outside the park makes it nice for my visits. While it may not be my go-to park because Lake Norman is so much closer to my home, I must admit, Stone Mountain remains my favorite.

New River State Park

New River State Park is located thirty-five miles northeast of Boone, NC. The Park offers seven access points along the shallow, gentle New River that flows north through three states. These separate park areas vary in accessibility, with some reachable by vehicle and others accessible exclusively by watercraft. Each of the seven river access points accommodates kayak and inner tube launches. The main park section, containing the office and drive-to campground, is located at the US221 Access. https://www.ncparks.gov/state-parks/new-river-state-park

The park's primary attraction is the New River. It is a very popular location for canoeing, kayaking, tubing, and fishing. This park accommodates all of those activities. In addition to these, visitors can also enjoy picnicking and engage in the ever-popular pastime of bird watching. There are also some hiking trails but the main activities are water based.

The park offers a variety of camping options, including backpacking or hike-in sites, paddle-in sites, group camping and drive-to tent and RV sites. The drive-to campground features twenty sites, some with only electrical hookups and others with full RV hookups. Unlike the separate sections at Stone Mountain, these sites are interspersed throughout the campground. The full hookup sites tend to be in higher demand, but all sites experience heavy usage during the warmer months, when river activities are most popular. The campground's terrain is somewhat hilly. Some sites have separate tiers for the parking area and the area with the table and fire ring. This requires navigating steps between the two areas, something to keep in mind if you have mobility issues. There is one handicap site.

Hiking options at the 221 Access are somewhat limited, with only two primary trails spanning a combined 2.4 miles. The Hickory Trail

(1 mile) can be accessed from the campground via the Campground Spur (0.28 miles) and connects to the River Run Trail (1.4 miles), which primarily follows the river's edge. All trails in the 221 Access are easy or moderate. There are more trails and some that are more strenuous in the other sections of the park. If you are interested in back country camping and backpacking, canoeing, paddle-to camping, primitive camping or strenuous hiking, you should explore the park's other sections by consulting the park website. It has excellent maps of each area and their features.

Various outfitters operate outside the park offering rental of watercraft and transportation to launch areas. There are launch locations at various distances from their base, depending on the package you choose. You will simply follow the current back to the original location to return the craft, get a snack and get back to camp. This section of the New River is well-suited to novice paddlers due to its shallow depth and gentle current.

If you're thinking about a float trip here, one thing you might want to do is inquire about the current water levels. Years ago, I took the boys on one of these trips. We rented two canoes. Because the weather had been very dry for several months, the river was very low causing our return to base to take much longer than we expected. We also kept running aground and, on a few occasions, had to move the canoes by hand for a few yards to get back underway. This experience is not representative of typical conditions.

Paddle Access / New River State Park

For those who prefer to remain on land and just want to camp and explore the area, there are many winding mountain roads in the area. The nearest town is Jefferson, about eleven miles away and then, the slightly larger West Jefferson. You can find most anything you need there. There's a decent downtown area in West Jefferson as well as in the smaller town of Lansing, nine miles up the road. There, you can visit the Creeper Trail Park for some easy walking, biking, fishing and other things. Near Jefferson, there is the Mount Jefferson State Natural Area which offers hiking, picnicking and scenic mountain overlooks.

For those who enjoy river-based activities, the New River State Park is an ideal destination. For those not into water sports, the park offers a pleasant camping experience and an opportunity to explore the surrounding area. It is an excellent area to escape the summer heat. The campground is newer than most state park campgrounds and it has very nice facilities. Electricity at every site makes for a comfortable stay. You might not have a signal, but your phone will be charged. The campground is a little small and can become busy at times. It is well-suited to accommodate both tent and small camper setups.

A visit to the New River State Park promises a memorable and enjoyable outdoor adventure. All in all, it's a nice place to camp and THE place if you want to get on the river. What if you are seeking a different experience? What if you're into something completely different, like, let's say horseback riding? Then South Mountains State Park is the place.

South Mountains State Park

This park is located approximately thirty miles south of Morganton, North Carolina. It is nestled at the point where the Appalachian Mountains give way to the foothills. There are two accesses to the park. The Clear Creek Access has some trails and a small lake. All other activities within the park are accessible through the Jacob Creek Access. The park offers hiking, biking, horseback riding, fishing and picnicking.   https://www.ncparks.gov/state-parks/south-mountains-state-park

The central focus of this park is equestrian activities. It features a campground equipped with stables, specifically designed for visitors who bring their horses. The Equestrian Campground offers fifteen sites, each with ample parking space to accommodate horse trailers. Additionally, the park boasts forty-seven miles of trails dedicated to horseback riding, with designated parking areas for horse trailers at both the Clear Creek and Jacob Creek accesses.

In addition to the Equestrian Campground, the park offers seven remote hike-to camp areas. The Family Campground, designed for both tents and RVs, provides a total of eighteen sites, some of which are equipped with electricity while others are not. The campground is furnished with a well-maintained bathhouse and several fresh water points. The Family Campground is somewhat small, and it should be noted that apart from a few exceptions, most of the sites are relatively small.

At the Clear Creek access, visitors can enjoy fishing and paddling on the lake. The Jacob Fork access features designated trout waters for fishing enthusiasts. The park also houses a visitor's center with various exhibits and essential items such as firewood and ice are available for purchase.

South Mountains State Park is rich in trails, offering twenty-seven trails of different uses over fifty miles. All trails are available for hiking, including the bridle trails. Several trails are designated for both biking and hiking. Four trails accommodate all three activities: hiking, biking, and horseback riding. From the campground you can hop on the half-mile, easy, River trail and access several other trials of varying intensity.

Scenic View / South Mountain State Park

If you feel the need to get out and about, be prepared for some travel. The somewhat winding, country roads can make the journey to civilization feel longer than it actually is. There is a well-stocked convenience store about 10 miles away on Highway 18. There may be one closer that I have not found. Once you make it that far, it's only about fifteen minutes up to Morganton. There, you can find most anything you might need. Heading in the opposite direction, you will encounter the town of Casar, NC. It's a pleasant town. I've been there many times with our Gospel group and have come to know many folks in that area. Salt of the earth people there.

Once you return to the park for a rest, you need not worry about your phone interrupting your nap. The campground is located in an area with absolutely no cell service. At the time of this writing, there is not a pay phone. I know pay phones are a thing of the past but in the other campgrounds where there is weak or no cell service, there is a pay phone for emergencies. Additionally, there is no WIFI available in the campground, an issue that I have politely raised concerns about. I emphasize 'politely' because, in my experience, the management of North Carolina state parks is excellent. In their defense, it should be noted that WIFI is accessible at the park office, which is a short distance away. However, as you head in that direction, you may experience a few bars of cell service just before reaching the office.

South Mountains is a very tranquil and picturesque park. It is also meticulously maintained and abundant in trails. It's an uplifting environment with the sight of horseback riders, wildlife, and the natural beauty of the surroundings. The campground is small, for sure. I had no issues securing a site during the week. The park's remote location contributes to its peacefulness. The lack of cell service is not a deal-breaker. It just slightly concerning from a safety perspective. If you want to a place to bring your horse to camp and ride, or you just want peace and quiet, this is the place. You won't be sitting around watching YouTube Camping Videos so bring along a book. But what if you need something that is convenient to town, offers easy access, and has a greater selection of campsites? That would lead you to Lake Norman.

Lake Norman State Park

Lake Norman State Park is located forty miles north of Charlotte, NC on the state's largest man-made lake. The park occupies a seventeen-mile stretch of shoreline and a smaller park lake for activities away from the busy, larger lake. The park is very convenient to a largely populated area and is well-utilized. The lakeshore includes a boat ramp and a pleasant swimming area with facilities. The park also provides hiking, biking, fishing, paddling and picnicking. https://www.ncparks.gov/state-parks/lake-norman-state-park

The park is popular for its Itusi Trail which comprises over thirty miles of mountain biking trails spread across eight separate loops. These trails are carefully designed, with many intersecting paths, providing a variety of biking experiences. It is important to note that biking and hiking trails are kept separate, and there are no bridle trails available for horseback riding.

The primary hiking trail at the park is the six-mile Lakeshore Trail. Most of it runs along the lakefront and is very scenic. For those desiring a shorter route, the Short Turn Trail can be utilized to cut the distance in half. Both trails are classified as moderate in intensity. The Lakeshore Trail can be easily accessed from both camping areas. Additionally, the park features the Alder Trail, a shorter trail of less than a mile designated as easy, as well as the handicap-accessible Butterfly Trail located near the Visitors Center.

I have had the pleasure of hiking the Lakeshore Trail on numerous occasions, both the full trail and the shortened version using the Short Turn Trail. It is well used and easy to follow. You won't get lost. Despite its popularity, the trail never seems crowded. You meet a few fellow hikers, but not many. And on some trips, you may even find yourself entirely alone. In those cases, you will likely startle a couple deer and see them dash off crashing through the woods.

The park lake offers fishing and boat rentals. It is a more low-key environment compared to the main lake, as it is separated by a dam. The park lake is conveniently situated near the Visitors Center, which houses exhibits, restrooms, and parking facilities.

For those interested in swimming, the park features a designated beach area on the main lake, complete with bathhouse facilities and ample parking.

For camping, the park offers two campgrounds, with no hike-to camping options available. The group campground provides tent camping facilities. The family campground consists of thirty-two tent sites without hookups and eleven RV sites with hookups. A dump station is provided for campers' convenience. Small RVs can be parked at tent sites, though some sites may not be ideally suited for this due to uneven driveways. Tents may also be set up on RV sites. Unfortunately, there are six "camper cabins" present, which can be seen as a contradiction in terms. In the section on reservations, we'll discuss how to choose a site away from these cabins. A single bathhouse is centrally located within the campground area.

Camping at the park is pleasant, with sites thoughtfully spaced out to ensure privacy. You can hear the lake sounds, boat motors, radios and water lapping the shore. It is not annoying and can be peaceful. Most tent pads are level and well-maintained, and all sites are well shaded. Drinking water sources are conveniently located near the tent sites, and the bathhouse is clean and comfortable.

Campsite by the lake / Lake Norman State Park

Getting out and about, you can easily locate a nearby convenience store and gas station for any necessary supplies. You can continue seven miles on to the small town of Troutman, which has a few stores and local restaurants The town also has nice parks, trails, natural space and miles of greenway to explore and enjoy.

If you are unable to find what you need in Troutman, the town of Mooresville is fifteen miles from the park. There you will find a wide array of big-box stores, restaurants, and a lively downtown area. The town is also home to several reputable antique stores and malls. Mooresville sometimes gets a bad rep for its heavy traffic volume. There's no way around it, (literally) it is busy. I have found that with a healthy dose of patience and a good application of the rules of the road, it's not nearly as daunting as it may initially seem. Try that, and you will get through just fine.

As I mentioned in the chapter describing the first trip, Lake Norman State Park is my preferred destination due to its proximity of less than thirty minutes from my home. It has all the features I need and plenty of additional attractions in the nearby area that I can visit. And, I know my way around the area. It also helps that I know which sites I prefer. All are good sites, but some are better than others. This is a nice park. It is busy but not necessarily crowded. It is roomy and peaceful without being remote.

Jordan Lake State Recreation Area

Seven access areas make this a recreation area instead of a single park. It is located thirty miles west of Raleigh, NC, on the Jordan Lake. The area offers camping, boating, fishing, swimming, hiking, paddling, and picnicking. The main feature is B. Everett Jordan Lake. It is 13,940 acres and has 180 miles of shoreline. https://www.ncparks.gov/state-parks/jordan-lake-state-recreation-area

Although the main attraction is the lake, considerable effort has been made to cater to camping enthusiasts. There are over 1,000 sites available across five access points. These include tent sites (including backpacking sites), RV sites (with some offering electric and water hookups), group tent sites (including backpacking sites), and group RV sites.

Since we are mostly concerned with drive-to sites, our options span four access areas: Crosswinds Campground, Parkers Creek Campground, Poplar Point Campground and Vista Point Campground. The first three offer both tent sites (non-electric) and RV sites (electric and water). They have ample facilities including bathhouses, beach area and boat launch. Many of the sites are located near the waterfront. Crosswinds Campground includes duplex sites for those who wish to camp with others. Vista Point Campground offers only full RV campsites with electric and water hookups. While this would typically suffice for tent camping, the absence of a bathhouse or restroom at Vista Point precludes tent camping in that area.

Once you are in place at your camp site, there are beach areas you can take advantage of. I have personally stayed at both Parkers Creek and Poplar Point campgrounds and used their respective beach areas which were well-maintained and not overly crowded. On one occasion, I even witnessed a mass baptism, which was quite an interesting experience.

Each campground features a hiking trail throughout the area for exercise and access from section to section.

Outside the park's boundaries, you'll find plenty of convenience stores and marinas. Traveling eight miles east on US 64, you'll arrive in Apex, where you can explore various big box stores, restaurants, and shops. Continuing approximately the same distance further will bring you to the Raleigh area. Raleigh, the state capital, offers numerous attractions and activities to enjoy. While you may not have come camping with the intention of exploring these urban attractions, the option is available. If you're a North Carolinian and have never visited the state capital, you should make plans to do so.

The campgrounds are nice and have good, level sites. The lake serves as a nice enhancement to the overall camping experience. With a variety of options available, it's generally possible to secure a site most of the time. It is not a remote location and can be somewhat busy at times. If you enjoy lake activities, it's an ideal location for camping. The nearby shopping options provide added convenience. The proximity to a large urban area increases the crowd at the park and reduces the park's quaintness. It's a suitable and accessible stop for those participating in The 7N7 Challenge.

And there you have it: nine state parks, which I have personally experienced, to choose from when creating your challenge. The state's Division of Parks and Recreation divides the state into three regions: Mountains, Piedmont, and Coastal. The parks I have reviewed are all located within the Piedmont and Mountains Regions, encompassing central and western North Carolina. Utilizing these parks makes it viable for me to complete the seven trips of the challenge.

There are numerous state parks located along the eastern edge of the Piedmont region and further east in the Coastal region, which offer drive-to tent camping. While I have not yet visited all of these parks,

I intend to do so in the future, potentially leading to the creation of another 7N7 Challenge guidebook.

Other Parks

Here is some information on the other state parks that offer drive-to camping.

Carolina Beach State Park

Carolina Beach State Park is located approximately twelve miles south of Wilmington, NC. The park is renowned for being the home of the Venus Flytrap, a fascinating carnivorous plant. In addition to the Venus Flytrap, the park features several interesting plant habitats. Among these is the Sugarloaf Dune, which stands fifty feet tall and was historically utilized by river pilots for navigation purposes. The park has a marina that serves the Intracoastal Waterway and the Cape Fear River. https://www.ncparks.gov/state-parks/carolina-beach-state-park

The campground offers two loops, each serviced by its own bathhouse and multiple water spigots. The loops collectively contain a total of eighty-three campsites, six of which are those unlikable cabins and nine sites that include electric power. Additionally, there are a few handicap-accessible sites and a dump station available for campers' convenience.

Three connecting trails from the campground connect it to eight of the nine hiking and walking trails in the park. These trails vary in length, ranging from a quarter-mile to three miles. All trails are designated as "Easy" in difficulty, with several of the trails being handicap-accessible. There is even a short, self-guided trail specifically designed for children, complete with activity brochures. The park website lists nine miles of hiking trails and one mile jef biking trails. The only biking trail is the Fitness Trail.

The Fitness Trail is a one-mile-long loop designed to be wheelchair accessible. Along the trail, you'll find several exercise and activity stations strategically placed to promote physical fitness. This trail is situated off 7th Street, with parking available at the Carolina Beach Recreation Center. Please be aware that the trail's surface is composed of gravel, and bicyclists should yield to hikers while using the trail.

A point of concern and clarification: While researching these parks during the time of writing, I discovered that some bike trails in certain parks were temporarily closed for maintenance. Also, I learned that bike trails can be difficult and expensive to maintain. This may have implications for the future of these trails in North Carolina parks. I don't know. As I am unable to predict the status of these trails, I make no guarantees regarding their presence or accessibility. For the folks who enjoy mountain biking while on their camping trips, I recommend checking trail status on the park's website before planning your visit.

If you are a beach lover, the Town of Carolina Beach is adjacent to the park. Here, you'll discover a plethora of activities, including a lively, old-fashioned seaside boardwalk featuring an arcade and various food options, such as pizza, donuts, and ice cream. You may rent a bike and explore the town, or simply bask in the sun and enjoy the surf. Travel a little further south and you can visit the Fort Fisher Historic Site where you will see the monuments and read about the history of the Civil War activities of the area. If history is not your thing, you can visit the Fort Fisher Aquarium where you can connect with aquatic wildlife.

Fort Fisher Historic Site

I have visited Carolina Beach many times over the years and have been in the park. The area is beautiful and provides a nice way to access both the old-time beach charm as well as the various waterway activities. For both experiences, the park is perfectly situated. The campground is heavily booked year-round and you will need to plan ahead. Oh, and also, make sure you pack some insect repellant as the area is known for its abundance of mosquitos.

Cliffs of the Neuse State Park

Cliffs of the Neuse is located fifteen miles southeast of the small town of Goldsboro, NC. The park rests on ninety-foot bluffs that overlook the Neuse River. The cliffs are composed of multiple layers of gravel, shale, sand, clay and seashells. The combination of mineral layers tints the face of the cliff in an array of complementing, natural colors. In addition to the river, there is an eleven-acre lake and several creeks surrounded by longleaf pine restoration areas. https://www.ncparks.gov/state-parks/cliffs-neuse-state-park

The park features a group camping area and a thirty-four-site, family campground. It offers seven full hookup sites and three camper cabins. One full hookup site and one cabin are handicap accessible. All sites are located in a single loop, served by a shared bathhouse and multiple water spigots.

Shady campsites / Cliffs of the Neuse State Park

The park has seven hiking trails totaling four miles. A spur trail connects the camping area to the overlook area, accessible via the 350 Yard Trail, which is the shortest and easiest route in the park. The Lake Trail, at 1.9 miles, is the longest and is rated moderate in difficulty.

The eleven-acre "Swim Lake" is centrally located in the park. It offers swimming, paddle boating, bathhouse and concession stand. Everything you need, right there. The park has, on occasion, closed the lake due to staffing shortages.

For canoeing or kayaking enthusiasts, the park offers The Neuse River Paddle Trail. The park maintains a launch site six miles upstream. Back at the park, there is a Sandbar accessible from the Spanish Moss Trail, designated as a canoe tie-up area, where one could stop and take a rest, I suppose. That is not a launch. But there is a paddling launch at the end of the 350 Yard Trail, by the Cliffs Overlook parking area. Two and a half miles downstream lies a Wildlife Resources boat ramp, marking the end of the 8.5-mile trip.

Sightings of river otters, eagles and various waterfowl are common along the Paddle Trail. The river provides abundant fishing opportunities. Under normal flow conditions, the entire trip typically takes around three hours to complete. That is unless you stop to fish, nap or snack. This stretch of the river is considered Moderate but the trip is recommended only for experienced paddlers. Paddlers are advised to check in at the park visitor center for the latest river conditions and to advise park staff of their float plan.

For the less adventurous paddler, canoes, kayaks, pedal boats, and stand-up paddleboards are available for rent, seasonally, for use on the Swim Lake.

A few small towns can be found near the park. However, if you need to acquire an item not commonly found at a dollar store, your best option is the outskirts of Goldsboro, located about twelve miles away. The town offers a variety of larger chain stores and restaurants. It also features a bustling downtown area. Check it out if you get out and about.

Falls Lake State Recreation Area

Located fifteen miles east of Durham, NC, Falls Lake Recreation Area encompasses the 12,410-acre Falls Lake Reservoir. The area provides seven access points for visitors to enjoy. A range of camping options is available, including tent, RV, backpacking, and group camping facilities. There are twenty-five miles of hiking trails, including a portion of the Mountains-to-Sea State Trail, and fourteen miles of biking trails. https://www.ncparks.gov/state-parks/falls-lake-state-recreation-area

Drive-to tent camping is offered in two accesses, Holly Point and Rolling View. Holly Point consists of five loops, each with its own bathhouse, and offers a total of 158 campsites. Of these, eighty-nine have water and power, while the remaining sites are standard tent sites. Rolling View has three loops with 115 campsites, eighty of which have water and power. The rest are typical tent sites. Both Holly Point and Rolling View have one handicap site per loop, but no cabins.

The Shinleaf campground offers forty-six hike-in tent sites, each equipped with a picnic table, outdoor grill, and lantern hook on the tent pad. A bathhouse is located near the entrance. Group camping sites are available at Rolling View, Shinleaf, and B.W. Wells, but require advance registration and are designated for tents only. Each site accommodates up to thirty-five people. Not all camping areas are open year-round.

Ten hiking-only trails are available, with some rated easy and others moderate. Additionally, there are five trails suitable for both hiking and biking, classified as intermediate or advanced biking. The Mountains-to-Sea State Trail can be accessed from the visitor center, Rolling View, or Shinleaf sections. The section of the trail that follows Falls Lake offers sixty miles of beautiful views.

The Beaverdam Lake section, separate from the main area of the lake, prohibits the use of gasoline motors, making it an ideal location for paddle sports. If you do not have your own equipment, rentals are available at the nearby Rolling View Marina.

Back on the main lake, there are public boat ramps at the Highway 50 and Rolling View accesses. B. W. Wells and Holly Point have boat ramps for campers only. Of course, there is the Marina located at Rolling View so all your boating needs are met.

Rolling View Marina / Falls Lake State Recreation Area

Falls Lake Recreation Area seems like a very large place with many features and activities. As I have not personally stayed or visited, I conducted research on reviews. I was not surprised to find very few negative reviews. Most were positive and referred to the place as sprawling, large, beautiful, and well maintained with well-spaced sites.

Goose Creek State Park

In the coastal region about 35 miles southeast of Greenville, you can find Goose Creek State Park. The park provides many coastal experiences including wetlands on the Pamlico River and a long boardwalk along a cypress swamp. Visitors can also observe remnants of the once-thriving lumber industry, such as a trackless railroad bed and old tar kilns. The park's picturesque landscape can be explored via hiking trails or paddling along the Pamlico River. https://www.ncparks.gov/state-parks/goose-creek-state-park

The park provides various camping options, including Primitive Camping, Group Camping, and Family Camping. For individual tent camping, visitors can choose between the Primitive and Family Camping areas. The Family Camping area features 22 full hookup sites, which include sewer connections and are more expensive. Each site comes with a tent pad. There is one handicap accessible site in this section, as well as one bathhouse. Additionally, six camper cabins are available for use, or to avoid, depending on personal preference.

The Primitive Camping area offers 14 tent sites that can accommodate two tents and two vehicles, meeting the criteria for a drive-to tent site. Water spigots are dispersed throughout this area, and, as the designation "primitive" suggests, there are composting toilets available but no bathhouse.

The park features 8.5 miles of hiking trails, including the boardwalk, and all are classified as easy. The trails vary in length, ranging from several 0.3-mile paths to the more remote Goose Creek Trail, which measures 2.5 miles long.

Palmetto Boardwalk / Goose Creek State Park

For paddling enthusiasts, Dinah's Landing serves as a launch site. However, it requires leaving and reentering the park on the opposite side of Goose Creek. This is the only designated launch site officially marked on the park map. However, according to reviews of the park's camping experience, there is another launch site near campsite 10 in the Family Camping Area, and potentially others along Goose Creek. Other park amenities include a swimming beach, as well as opportunities for fishing, picnicking, and birdwatching.

In order to experience the historic flavor of the area, a visit to nearby small towns of Bath and Washington is recommended. Bath, established in 1705, holds the distinction of being North Carolina's oldest town and first port. It hosts several historic sites as well as quaint local shops. The drive from the park to Bath is a scenic journey worth taking, especially with the charming Bath as the destination.

Gorges State Park – Grassy Ridge Access

Gorges State Park is situated in the southwestern corner of North Carolina, where the borders of North Carolina, South Carolina, and Georgia converge. As the name implies, the park features deep river gorges with twenty-six waterfalls and sheer rock precipices. The park offers various backcountry style recreation including horseback riding, backpacking, hiking, and camping. The park borders part of Lake Jocassee, Pisgah National Forest and the Toxaway Game Lands. Covering 8000 acres of rainforest, the park has two accesses. It hosts several miles of the Foothills Trail, a seventy-six-mile National Recreation Trail in South and North Carolina. https://www.ncparks.gov/state-parks/gorges-state-park

The secondary access and entrance to Gorges State Park is Frozen Creek, which offers a parking area and restrooms for picnicking and access to most of the hiking and bridle trails. The primary access and entrance is Grassy Creek. From there you can access the Visitors Center, Picnic Shelter, and the drive-to camping area.

For camping, the park offers several backcountry campsites, reachable by hiking or horseback. The main campground features sixteen tent sites, one of which is handicap accessible, and fourteen RV sites, with one being handicap accessible as well. Additionally, there are five crusty camping cabins, one that is handicap accessible.

The park website boasts of fifty-six miles of hiking trails, seventeen miles of biking trails and twelve miles of horseback riding trails. However, upon examining the maps and trail listings, it appears that the actual total is approximately half of that. It is a very large park and no doubt I am overlooking something. Either way there is plenty of room to hike, bike or ride on a variety of trails rated from easy to strenuous. There is no trail directly accessed from the drive-to camping area.

Trailhead / Gorges State Park

Reviewers describing the camping experience at Gorges remark that the park is very clean and new, with numerous hiking trails and waterfalls to explore. They emphasize the peaceful atmosphere of the park and the well-kept, nice facilities.

The park is in close proximity to Lake Toxaway and all of the associated, essential establishments. Outside the park you can find convenience and dollar stores nearby. While the unincorporated community of Cashiers has some commercial establishments, the nearest town or city of significant size is Brevard. It will take you about thirty minutes to get there but you can find anything you need in that area.

In fall of 2023, it was reported that a black bear ripped the sides off of a travel trailer at the Gorges State Park campground. There was a photo of the camper that was widely circulated on social media. The camper in the photograph was so severely damaged that it appeared to be a hoax or myth. However, the occurrence was actually true and the photo originated from the NC Parks social media. As a result of the incident, officials closed the campground for two weeks, cancelled reservations, and issued refunds. They also issued guidance and warnings. This is a concern and human contact with a black bear is a real possibility. Familiarize yourself with the safety steps and official information before camping at Gorges.

Jones Lake State Park

Jones Lake State Park is located about forty miles southeast of Fayetteville. Jones Lake and nearby Salters Lake are known as Carolina Bays. These elliptical to circular depressions are a geological mystery and the origins are unknown. The lake's maximum depth is only eight feet, but its tea-colored water gives the illusion of greater depth. In addition to camping, the park offers swimming, picnicking and hiking. https://www.ncparks.gov/state-parks/jones-lake-state-park

Camping options at Jones Lake State Park include group camping, tent and RV camping. The tent and RV campground features twenty sites, with six offering full RV hookups—including water, electricity, and sewer—while the remaining fourteen are non-electric sites, suitable for tent camping or RV boondocking. There is a price difference between the two types of sites, and reservations are recommended.

For hiking enthusiasts, the four-mile Bay Trail, rated Moderate, circles Jones Lake and links to the one-mile Salters Lake trail, which connects the two lakes. Additionally, there is an easy-rated, one-mile Cedar Loop Trail connected to the Bay Trail.

The park features a swimming area, a boat ramp, a boat house with seasonal boat rentals and concession stand, and a fishing pier.

There are convenience stores within five miles of the park. Elizabethtown is six minutes from the park and provides restaurants and grocery stores.

A consensus of online reviews of the park campground describes it as clean, well-cared for and quiet. While the park is a popular local destination, it can also serve as an excellent location for a quiet camping trip. Due to the limited number of campsites, advanced planning and reservations are recommended.

Kerr Lake Recreation Area

This recreation area occupies two counties along the state's border with Virginia. The 50,000-acre lake hosts eight access areas that include seven campgrounds with hundreds of campsites. Each access area provides a boat ramp. In addition to camping and boating, visitors can enjoy hiking, paddling, swimming, fishing, picnicking, and birdwatching.   https://www.ncparks.gov/state-parks/kerr-lake-state-recreation-area

Of the eight access areas, seven offer drive-to camping, with both electric and non-electric sites available. Each area also has limited double sites, as well as bathhouses and dump stations. Some sites are situated near the shoreline, while others are not as close. Group camping is available in some areas, but there are no cabins. A comprehensive park map in PDF format displays all areas and campsites, allowing you to choose from hundreds of options.

Of course, the primary attraction of this park is the lake and the associated activities. There are three miles of trails for hiking enthusiasts, and fishing piers can be found at Bullocksville and Henderson Point. As the park website notes, "Not every access has all the listed facilities", so check the park map to help in your planning.

Outside the park, there are a couple of convenience stores in close proximity. The small town of Middleburg is a short distance away, offering a restaurant and a dollar store. A few miles further, the city of Henderson provides access to most major chain stores and restaurants.

With electric, non-electric, double sites, handicap sites and group sites, there are plenty of camping options at Kerr Lake. Reservations may not be needed but would be recommended if you want to be in a particular area with a particular type of site.

Raven Rock State Park

Raven Rock State Park is situated about forty miles southwest of Raleigh, near the small town of Lillington, NC. The park is divided by the picturesque Cape Fear River, with bridle trails and horse trailer parking on one side and all other amenities on the other. The main access provides parking for the Visitors Center, picnic areas and hiking trails featuring captivating points of interest, such as the 150-foot crystalline structure known as Raven Rock, which overlooks the river. https://www.ncparks.gov/state-parks/raven-rock-state-park

The campground, biking trails, and their respective parking areas are accessed via a separate road from the main area to minimize congestion. The campground features a single loop with twenty-four campsites. These include nine equipped with power, water, and sewer connections, and fifteen tent sites suitable for both tents and large RVs, though without hookups. A centrally located bathhouse serves the campground. Additionally, there are six camper cabins available for those who...well for those who desire to stay in a cabin. The park also has backpack camping with both hike-in and paddle-in sites.

Park Entrance / Raven Rock State Park

The campground facilities are relatively new and nicely done. Even the cabins look nice, for now. The tent pads are larger than those found in some parks, and all sites are fairly level. This campground is meticulously cared for and constantly pristine. I had the opportunity to camp there as this book was nearing completion, and was very impressed. A detailed description will be featured in the next 7N7 Challenge book.

The hiking trails at the park range from easy to moderate, with lengths varying from 0.2 miles to 4.6 miles. The Raven Rock Loop Trail is 2.6 miles and designated easy. However, there is a point where you can go down a long set of steep stairs to the riverfront to view the rockface. That stair climb is not part of the easy trail. The trail also includes an overlook offering panoramic views of the river area, although the rockface is not visible from this vantage point. The moderate Fish Traps

Trail leads to the Fish Trap rapids and the remnants of the Northington Lock and Dam. For a longer hike, Campbell Creek Loop will take you to the primitive camping area and to the Lanier rapids via the 0.2-mile Lanier trail.

Bikers can enjoy three interconnected loops catering to beginner, intermediate, and advanced skill levels, allowing for extended rides by combining loops. These bike trails are accessed via the same road as the campground and have their own designated parking area.

There is at least one launch area and various points for fishing. There is a large picnic shelter near the trailheads located at the main entrance.

There are two bridle trails in the Avent's Creek Access area. Both are four-mile trials. There is parking in the area to accommodate horse trailers.

For those seeking activities outside the park, the nearby town of Lillington offers a small shopping strip containing an old-fashioned hardware store, grocery store, gun shop, and pharmacy, providing all essential amenities in one convenient location. Lillington's downtown area features unique shops, while larger city attractions can be found in Fuquay-Varina, just thirteen miles away.

Raven Rock State Park provides an excellent camping experience, with a diverse range of activities and points of interest available for visitors. The area is serene, and the campground is well-maintained and comfortable. It is a highly recommended destination to visit and check off your list for the 7N7 Challenge.

Merchants Millpond State Park

Merchants Millpond State Park is nestled 10 miles south of the state's northeastern border with Virginia in Gates County, North Carolina. The park's crowning feature is a historic, 190-year-old, millpond. At 760 acres, the Millpond serves as the centerpiece of this interesting wetland environment. Visitors can enjoy hiking the surrounding trails or paddling the calm, shallow waters of the pond to explore the area's natural beauty. The park's Lassiter Swamp features old-growth cypress trees adorned with Spanish moss, creating an enchanting atmosphere. Visitors may even catch a glimpse of the American alligator, as the park marks the northernmost point of its range. https://www.ncparks.gov/state-parks/merchants-millpond-state-park

For camping, the park offers a variety of options, including individual and group hike-in and paddle-in camping. For drive-to camping there is a group campground and a family campground. The family campground has a single bathhouse serving only twenty sites, and all are non-electric. There is no dump station.

There are over sixteen miles of hiking trails, all rated easy. This includes the bicycle trail, a five-mile loop that is also open to hikers. In addition to those trails, the park has a unique system of paddle trails. These include about two miles of paddling on the main pond and several miles of floating on Bennetts Creek.

The park has several picnic areas, restrooms and offers fishing, a launch area, boat ramp and canoe rentals.

Folks who have visited the park describe the campground as very nice with level, wooded and private sites. Those who have visited for a day trip are impressed with the beauty and the excellent paddling experience offered by the calm water, which one reviewer described as "like paddling on black glass". The most frequent advice seems to be to make preparations for many mosquitos.

There are two convenience stores near the park and a dollar store in Gatesville which is about five miles away. There are no cities nearby. If you are looking for some points of interest outside the park you will have to do some travelling. Sometimes the journey itself is the experience. I'll leave it to you to find your own destination.

Merchant's Millpond State Park will make a great stop for a 7N7 Challenge. All indications are that it would be especially fun for someone ready to get into paddling but not ready for rapid waters. The campground is peaceful and small. Reservations may be needed. Be prepared for bugs.

William B. Umstead State Park

William B. Umstead State Park, located approximately ten miles northwest of Raleigh, serves as an excellent escape from the harried pace of urban life. The park features numerous trails suitable for hiking, biking, and horseback riding. Fishing enthusiasts can enjoy the park's three man-made lakes. Both park entrances provide picnic areas and shelters for visitors. For those seeking a rustic experience, the historic Maple Hill Lodge offers an alternative to camping.

As of this writing, the campground at William B. Umstead State Park is temporarily closed for renovations. Upon further investigation, it appears that the upgrades will consist of a new bathhouse and enhancements to the campsites. There is currently no estimated date for the campground's reopening. Once the campground reopens, I intend to plan a camping trip there, which will be featured in a future 7N7 Challenge and book.

Chapter Five / Making Reservations

The easiest way to reserve your campsite is to visit the website of the park you wish to visit. Navigate to the "Camping" section, where you will find a link to book online and a phone number for those who prefer to make reservations by phone. Personally, I prefer making reservations online. The state uses Reserve America for this purpose. You will need to create an account to proceed. Clicking on the "Reserve Online" link will either direct you to a sign-in page or the reservation page for the specific park you are interested in.

Upon reaching the reservation page, you will be prompted to enter your arrival dates and length of stay. You can narrow down your search to a specific type of site or a specific loop in the campground. There is an interactive map to the right side of the page. All sites that are available, using your criteria, will be displayed in blue. All unavailable sites will be displayed in tan. If you want to avoid being near something, such as a cabin, or want to be near something such as a bathhouse, you can refer to the map for guidance. Clicking on a site will open a small popup containing a picture and some information about the site. For more details, click on the popup, and a new page will load, providing additional information, including a timeline of the site's availability. Occasionally, more photographs are included and will have the option to book the site. If the site does not meet your preferences, you can click on another site in the small map on that page or use your browser's back button to return to the previous page and start over.

There is a small fee for reserving online. There are several policies related to making reservations that may change periodically. As a result, my advice is to familiarize yourself with the current policies on the park's website or the Reserve America site.

Cancellations can be made online up to the day before the scheduled arrival date. Plan on forfeiting some of your refund. Cancellations made on the scheduled arrival date will result in the forfeiture of one night's camping fees for each reservation and the reservation fee and transaction fee. No refunds for no-shows or for cancellations or early departures after the date of arrival. The policies are made clear and must be agreed to upon making the reservation. They will also be forwarded to you in the confirmation email.

These cancellation policies are, in my opinion very reasonable, and possibly too lenient. The growing popularity of camping has made it increasingly challenging to get a reservation. As a result, some individuals book multiple sites months in advance, without being certain they will use them, only to cancel at the last minute for the sake of convenience. This issue frustrates campers attempting to find a site closer to the date of their trip. I have experienced the frustration of searching multiple parks before locating an available site, only to arrive and discover numerous vacant sites. This is bad for state park camping, and is a hot topic of discussion among campers I talk to. I don't know the ideal solution but cancellation policies might be a good place to start.

Currently, you can make reservations up to six months in advance. When booking online, you must secure your reservation at least one day before your arrival. So far, I have only needed to cancel twice. I have had success waiting until the day before my arrival to make my reservation, as it allows me to have a better understanding of the weather conditions. On a few occasions, however, by reserving late, I had to choose a different park than the one I wanted.

As I may have previously mentioned, it is possible to secure a campsite by arriving at the campground and choosing from what is available. Each park has a large sign at the campground entrance that posts that park's procedures for this approach and occasionally, a list of available sites. However, I would only recommend this method if you are well-acquainted with the park and reasonably confident that a site will be available

Reserved Campsite / Pilot Mountain State Park

When making your reservation, if you have a choice of sites, it is important to make as good a choice as possible. Your time is precious. You are spending your hard-earned money to enjoy a relaxing time. There are some things that might need to be taken into consideration. First consider if it is important for you to be near the bathhouse. If so, make that a priority in your choice. If you are like me and enjoy solitude, look for a site that is more isolated. These will usually be the sites further from amenities. Typically, the more peaceful sites are located on the outside of the loop and not the inside. If the distance you must carry water is of concern to you, the park campground maps indicate where the water spigots are located.

Although parks have a quiet hour, your stay can be easily ruined by loud or rowdy neighbors. This can happen at any site at any park. You can complain, but by then you might already be too disappointed to enjoy your trip. I always bring earplugs for this possibility. In my experience, occupants of camping cabins, as a general rule, are louder than those who are camping in equipment they purchased, maintained, set up and in which they have a little pride of ownership. In my humble opinion, if you want peaceful neighbors, you might choose a site away from cabins.

If you have a question about any site or regulation or procedure, you can call the park. You can also send a message on the park contact page. I did this one time and got a very prompt and polite response. As I said, North Carolina does a good job managing parks. Don't be intimidated by the reservation process. The days of just showing up and expecting to find a campsite have almost passed us by. Making a reservation is the best way to go. Once you get your account established and go through the process, you will find that Reserve America is easy to navigate.

Chapter Six / Finding Things to Do

As much as it would please those of us who are less inclined to do anything beyond sit around and relax, we need to engage in some activity beyond just hanging around camp. When I used to take the boys camping, I did all the cooking and most of the cleaning. It was the type of thing that was easier for me to do myself than to instruct them how to do it and expect it to get done to my satisfaction. I often took a day, while they were out fishing or tubing all day, to stay by the cook fire, so to speak. Between meals I would read a book or take a nap. It is a sure-fire stress reliever to have a day like that.

The truth is, unless there is someone else around to carry on a conversation, just sitting around camp all day can get almost boring after a while. On all my 7N7 Challenge trips, I went alone. So, I needed to get out and about. All of the parks I chose had hiking trails. As we saw in the parks section, there are other activities as well, but there is always a place to hike or walk. You might go fishing, rock climbing, biking, swimming. There are options. But if nothing else, even if you are not into hiking, I promise you will appreciate a good hike or walk and it will make you feel good once you are back in camp.

Trail Marker, Grindstone Trail / Pilot Mountain State Park

If biking, swimming, kayaking, or fishing are more to your liking, plan accordingly and bring the proper gear. Check out each park's activities ahead of time and decide what you might need. But remember, more gear means more stuff to pack, keep up with, and unpack. Walking or hiking takes very little added equipment.

If you are a musician like me, playing your instrument in the solitude of the outdoors can be a great way to hone your skills. I almost always bring along a banjo. Most of the time, you will be entertaining yourself, so there is no pressure, and you can experiment outside the box and enjoy the time. One word of caution here: instruments can be very expensive. If you have been playing any time at all, you will know this. Don't bring an expensive instrument on your camping trip. There are too many opportunities for it to get damaged or destroyed. At the same time, you want it to be fun, so don't bring one that is so cheaply made that it will frustrate your playing. Find a decent, entry-level instrument that works, one that you won't cause you to panic and reach into a campfire to save it from destruction.

When I was taking the boys on camping trips, we always brought instruments and sat around playing. One kid was especially talented. He played an inexpensive but well-built guitar and he played almost constantly. When he stopped, he laid it directly on the ground. It had scars and dirt and burn marks all over it but it still played. I asked him about it years later and he still had the guitar and still used it.

Banjo Pickin' Time

On a two-night trip, you have roughly half a day once you arrive, then one full day, then you will leave the next morning. While I might take a walk or hike the first evening, I usually plan a good one for the morning of the middle day. After that, I get cleaned up, and head out to explore and find something of interest outside the park.

I've never had any trouble finding something outside of the park. Each park is located where it is for a reason. Whatever that reason - lake, mountain, beach, etc., guarantees that that area of the country is also interesting. If you are like me, just poking around the nearest small town can be fun. Downtown areas are sometimes fascinating. An antique store will almost always have some interesting old-school camping gear. You could even find a good restaurant and eat out for your second supper of the trip. It sort of defeats the purpose and fun of camping, but still, it could add to the adventure of it. Seven restaurants in seven towns? No challenge there.

Once I arrive back at camp, I usually settle down for the previously much-talked-about nap. I might bring out the banjo and pick some, hoping nobody gets frustrated hearing it. An evening stroll through the campground is VERY interesting. Especially if you are into people watching. You will see every type of camping configuration from someone sleeping in their tiny car to an elaborate hammock system to a diesel pusher motor home.

The motor home people, who have a luxurious place to sit inside, will be sitting outside watching a television on the side of the rig while close by, someone who is staying in a tent, will be sitting in their car watching videos on their tablet. If you see someone in a cheap tent with a huge tarp stretched out over it, you are witnessing someone who has been disappointed on a past rainy trip because they didn't prepare ahead of time with some waterproofing. All in all, most people know what they're doing and are camping the way they prefer it, and it's interesting to see.

If you enjoy lounging and reading or spending time on social media, a campsite is a peaceful place to do that. Make sure you bring your reader or tablet and a way to keep it charged. If you prefer real books to e-books, you will need good reading light if you plan on reading at night. There are some campgrounds where you will have neither Wi-Fi nor a phone signal. An old standard paperback book and a flashlight might be your best friends. It would pay to have an emergency book packed away in your regular camping bag or pack.

Finding things to do is usually not a problem. Keep in mind any health limitations you have when planning the physical activities. Even with the best planning, you can end up stuck in a tent or vehicle for some time during a rain storm. Plan ahead for something to occupy your time when that happens. Bring along a magazine or maybe a notepad to scribble out your plan for the next adventure. In the next section, we will help in the planning stage.

Chapter Seven / Planning / Challenge

There is a reason the title of this chapter is divided. My original thought was to include a chapter on planning and another one to sort of wrap things up. However, after getting to this point in the book, you probably already have a plan in your mind. So, we won't get too deep into that but will simply recap some highlights. Then we'll finish up with some words of encouragement.

Planning a challenge starts as simply as coming up with a general, overall plan and becomes slightly more complicated when working out the details of each individual trip. The place to start is getting your gear together, as we discussed in Chapter Two.

For gear, if you are an experienced camper, you likely already have what you need. If not, use what you have and add to it as needed. For example, if you have no sleeping bag but own a sheet and blanket, start with that if you want. Starting from complete scratch with all new stuff can be a little costly. I have found good used camping equipment at thrift stores. I have loaned camping gear out to folks many times. Maybe someone you know could help you out. Another problem with purchasing all your gear upfront is you can end up making choices that would be better made after gaining hands-on experience to know what suits you best.

As I might have mentioned, you will forget something. A single-night trial run in the backyard will help avoid a lot of that. The two most popular items I have loaned out, frequently, to other campers are a can opener and a lighter.

Once your gear is in place, the rest simply requires taking logical steps:

- **Where and when**: Pick some parks near your home in areas you are familiar with. Maybe take advantage of the suggestions in Chapter Four, or find some place on your own;
- **Make reservations**: Don't be intimidated by the reservation process. Even though the procedure changes from time to time, Chapter Five will guide you well. I suggest making reservations only one trip at a time. If it is your preference, or your schedule requires that you plan your dates far in advance, prepare yourself to occasionally endure some bad weather. On the other hand, if you prefer good weather and have a flexible schedule, you can hold off reserving a site until a few days out. In that case, you might have trouble finding a site in your intended location and might have to choose a secondary location. You make it work to fit your situation. After a time or two, your procedure will become obvious and second nature. I say: watch the weather and go for it.
- **Create a menu**: Get the food together from your menu (refer to my menu planning section in Chapter Two), pack everything up and head out. A quick tip here: don't forget some snacks but don't overdo it. Camping makes you hungry.
- **Pack and go:** Once you have it all packed, you will be surprised at how much stuff you have. You will start almost immediately planning ways to downsize your kit. Don't stress, enjoy the trip, even the drive.

We're getting down to the short rows here. Maybe some of my personality has become obvious through these pages. Listen, I know myself. I know that I like solitude, that I don't like cabins in campgrounds, and that I can be grouchy. I prefer a non-crowded camping experience. I also know that camping can ease stress and worry in your life, and I want that for you, even if it means more people in the campgrounds I use often.

I live in a rural area. Friends my age who have lived all their lives in town or close to town in a subdivision are looking for land in the country to relocate. Americans, in general, are leaving urban areas and moving to rural areas. This is known as rural flight or counterurbanization. It has been happening for decades but was kicked into overdrive by Covid. High living costs, crime rates, overcrowding, and just the hectic way of life are partly to blame. Many people are looking for a better quality of life and a closer connection to nature. I believe that with everything going on these days, folks just need a more peaceful surrounding in which to relax. Camping can bring you closer to that, even if you can't relocate right now.

I am convinced that most people who need this peaceful return to nature, would never do it unless they encounter a device or plan to spur them on. A personal challenge might just be the key. My challenge to you is to go out and challenge yourself to series of outdoor adventures. Create a method that pushes you to a campsite in the great outdoors.

Sunset at camp / Goose Creek State Park

As a Christian, I would be remiss if I didn't warn you that, while this kind of peace is needed in this world, it is fleeting. There is another peace that passes understanding, which can only be found through a relationship with Jesus. Allow me to give you a brief break from the world, and a nugget from the Word, that perhaps presents another challenge, a more important one:

Romans 5:1 Therefore being justified by faith, we have <u>peace</u> with God through our Lord Jesus Christ: 2 By whom also we have access by faith into this grace wherein we stand, and rejoice in hope of the glory of God. 3 And not only so, but we glory in tribulations also: knowing that tribulation worketh patience; 4 And patience, experience; and experience, hope: 5 And hope maketh not ashamed; because the love of God is shed abroad in our hearts by the Holy Ghost which is given unto us. 6 For when we were yet without strength, in due time Christ died for the ungodly. 7 For scarcely for a righteous man will one die: yet peradventure for a good man some would even dare to die. 8 But God commendeth his love toward us, in that, while we were yet sinners, Christ died for us.

For more information, go to BillyGraham.org and click on "Start Your Journey Today[1]"

So, back to camping. You decide. What will it be? Will you take on a challenge exactly like mine, or create your own? Do you need some suggestions? Oh, you want seven?

How about an easier challenge:

- Seven visits to state parks in seven months, some camping and some day trips.
- Seven single nights camping in seven state parks.
- Seven day hikes in seven state parks.

---

1. https://peacewithgod.net/steps/?

- Maybe you don't have the equipment together yet, or have limited time, or just want to ease into it. Then make short visits to seven state parks in seven months or seven weeks, and just check them out. While there, you can make notes on which sites you will use in the future. In the meantime, you can get things worked out for a bigger challenge.

Need something more challenging?

- Seven camping trips in any number of state parks, in seven months.
- My next challenge is going to be: seven state parks that I have not camped in, in seven months. Stay tuned for that book.
- Here's a tougher one, the retired person's special: Camp in seven state parks in seven different states in seven months!

Make it fit your situation, but make it a real challenge. It needs to be a little tough. When you complete it, of course you will relish your accomplishment. But the real fun happens along the way... the way you might not have taken if you hadn't challenged yourself. The planning and plotting will be fun as well.

For those of you who, for whatever reason, are not able to actually go camping but like to read about the adventures, watch for my next book. It will be almost entirely about the actual trips I made on the next challenge and contain very little boring technical information. The book will be filled with the stories of seven trips to seven parks that I had never visited before. A challenge for sure, but great fun!

I have to be honest here. When I first designed The 7N7 Challenge and set out to do it, I did not complete it. That's right, I am writing about something I failed at, sort of. What I accomplished was creating an experience that was a very fulfilling and fun time that I will always remember.

I was on my fifth trip. I had a real cool site in Morrow Mountain State Park. I had a good hike, a good meal, and one good night's sleep. 8AM, my phone rang. It was time for my grand twins to be born. So, I packed up and headed home. With all the excitement and activity of having twin grandbabies, camping left my mind completely and I didn't make a trip the next month. I came back for trip number six in October, which was the seventh month, but didn't get seven trips completed in seven months. Life happens, sometimes even in a good way. Babe Ruth once said "Don't let the fear of striking out keep you from playing the game."

When I began writing this book, I knew I would try again. In the meantime, I kept camping...frequently. Then one day I started counting and realized I had just completed Seven trips in Seven months. I repeated one park once and I did a South Carolina Park for one of the seven trips. Not exactly the original challenge but a good encouragement for me to take it up again. More to come.

The point is, don't overstress about it. Stay safe; have fun! Dare to Get Out There.

About the Author

Jeff McCorkle is a retired Deputy Sheriff with a deep passion for the outdoors. His lifelong love for camping inspired him to develop the 7N7 Challenge, a personal initiative that encourages exploration and adventure. This challenge ignited his desire to share his experiences through writing. As he continues to expand his writing series beyond his debut, Jeff draws on his law enforcement background and his travels as the band leader of a Bluegrass Gospel band to enrich his storytelling. His unique perspective allows him to offer practical advice to fellow outdoor enthusiasts seeking to enhance their experiences in nature.